Calvin And The Magic Formula

Michelle Green

Illustrated By Amita Bhat

Copyright © Michelle Green 2024
All Rights Reserved.

ISBN
Paperback 979-8-89544-805-2
Hardcase 979-8-89588-970-1

I dedicate this book to my Dad, Mom and Brother

who left my world, too early in my life.

A special thank you to

Franchelle Raj for being a wonderful friend and
support through this entire process,

Annamaria Ronca for always making time to offer me advice and help through my
journey, and

Amita Bhat for being such a gifted illustrator who was very prompt and always
went above and beyond

1.
Wondering what was wrong

It was a beautiful day with perfect weather to come out and play. Yet, Calvin the carrot and Amna the apple looked sad.

Why were their friends looking so pale and tired? They didn't come out to play with them anymore.

Back in the day, every morning Calvin and Amna's friends would play hide and seek with them, bright and full of energy.

Recently though, these same friends seemed all worn out and drained.
Would those old fun days ever come back?

Calvin and Amna lived together with the rest of their family.

There was Mummy Carol the Cabbage, and Daddy Pablo the Pumpkin.

They had lots of brothers and sisters too, who were all well looked after by Mrs. Yuki.

2.

Mrs. Yuki's garden

Their home, the garden, was often visited by Mrs. Yuki's friends. Everyone would always say how lovely Calvin, Amna and their family looked.

Why were things so different in their friends' garden, they wondered.

3.

Mr Gray's garden

Calvin and Amna's friends lived in
Mr. Gray's garden.

Mr. Gray was a very busy man.
He did not have the time to care
for his garden like Mrs. Yuki.

Every morning he would just put the
water irrigation on and leave for work.

 4.

What can we do to help our friends?

Calvin said, "We need to do something about it!", Amna was curious about what her little brother had in mind.

Calvin decided, "We could sneak into Mrs. Yuki's house and see what she does every day".

Amna wasn't sure what he meant.

"We need to learn more about what Mrs. Yuki does, that helps keep us so strong and healthy", Calvin explained.

20

5.

The kitchen

"While Mrs. Yuki cooks, she saves all the food scraps,"
Calvin noticed. "She never throws them in the trash!"

Amna wondered where Mrs. Yuki saved her food
scraps. She thought it would make the kitchen messy.

"You won't believe it, but she turns it into something incredibly valuable!", Calvin exclaimed.
SCRAPS

"She saves the scraps in a small bin beneath her kitchen sink", Calvin explained what he saw.
COMPOST
25

6.

What are you doing in my kitchen?

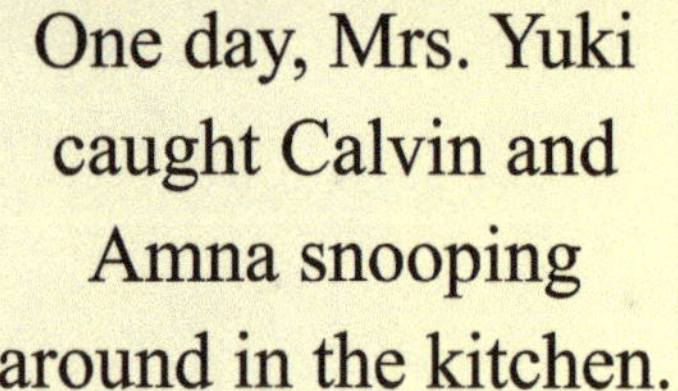

One day, Mrs. Yuki caught Calvin and Amna snooping around in the kitchen.

"What are you two doing in my kitchen?", she asked in an annoyed manner.

They went on to say how worried they were about their friends in Mr. Gray's garden.

They missed spending time with them. They were not coming out to play anymore as they were wilting and didn't have any energy, like before.

7.

The magic formula - Compost!

Mrs. Yuki was really
worried too.

She told them all about
the things she did to keep
Calvin, and his family
healthy and looking fresh
all the time.

Mrs. Yuki, very
cheerfully and proudly
said, "I feed all of you
the magic formula -
compost!"

What is this "Compost",
wondered Calvin!

"Saving the old, stinky food scraps
and keeping them over time, stored
in a bin, turns it into compost?"

A Poem on Compost

Compost Pile

In the garden, by the trees,
Lives a magic pile that everyone sees.
We call it compost, brown and green,
It makes our world fresh and clean.
**

Apple cores and carrot tops,
Leaves and grass in big, big drops,
Eggshells, paper, veggie peels,
In the compost, it all heals.
**

Worms and bugs, they love to munch,
Turning scraps to soil for lunch.
Mix it, stir it, let it lay,
Compost grows a bit each day.
**

Watch it crumble, dark and sweet,
Nourishing plants from root to leaf.
Flowers bloom and veggies grow,
Thanks to compost, just so you know!
**

So gather scraps, don't throw away,
Start a compost pile today.
Nature's cycle, round and round,
Making magic in the ground.

8.

What is composting?

"Composting is like making a special sandwich for the tiny creatures that live in the dirt", explained Mrs. Yuki

She went on to say, "We can layer food scraps, old leaves, grass clippings, and other things from the garden in a pile, like bread and filling in a sandwich.

It's like adding the lettuce and tomatoes in a sandwich!

As the tiny worms and other creatures chomp away, they turn all the scraps into special dirt that helps plants grow well".

Activity Page

COMPOSTING

WORD SEARCH

Find the words listed below and mark them in different colours.

```
T T Z X W A S T E O G D J L
D S A C X P A Y N S O S N S
J O D L M H F V C O K P Z L
V P L P U J H R F I C M Y E
M M I L S M A K T N Y A I E
E O O A K P R C W S Z G V P
A C S N S B H O E V J I Z H
R I Y T Y E G Y F Y Z C E Q
T N P S N G P Y I U W Z Z M
H D E L B A T E G E V O Y E
Z J B D A Y T O T E T T A K
N K E J R N F S Q Z Z H K L
Z Z S S N A E T A W U K G Y
X J V B I N G T D J J J F T
```

- BIN
- FOOD
- KITCHEN
- COMPOST
- SCRAPS
- WASTE
- PLANTS
- PLANET
- SOIL
- PEELS
- FORMULA
- GARDEN

9.
Every BIT counts

"I'm still not sure what compost is made of", whined Amna.

Turn to the next pages and help Amna understand better, what compost is made of.

Calvin was thrilled! "We can play with our friends again, because when we feed them our compost, they will get strong and healthy."

"We can start our play dates once more!", he screamed with excitement.

Activity Page

Colour in the circle against the items that you think are good to add to making compost

Apple core

Red pepper

Toilet roll tubes

Veggie peels

Cardboard

Tea bag

Plastics

Trainers

10.
About Mrs. Yuki

Amna liked how Mrs. Yuki was so thoughtful and caring. Mrs. Yuki remembered how her Mum and Dad taught her to love and respect the land they lived on.
Dad would do the gardening, raking those dried leaves and piling them up. These were added to all the food scraps that Mum would have, after she finished cooking.

They would use the compost to put back into their garden soil and eat those very fruits and vegetables which grew in their backyard.

Mrs. Yuki as a child, was always taught to treasure nature and wildlife and to handle every living thing with care.

11.
Planet earth

Humans are not the only living creatures on the planet.

Size Comparison

We are just a tiny bit of a bigger picture that helps make it all complete.

Lesson Plan

Introduction to composting

Objective:

To teach young children the basics of composting and the importance of recycling organic waste to help the environment.

Materials Needed:

- ☑ Calvin and the Magic formula book on composting
- ☑ Small compost bin or clear container for demonstration
- ☑ Organic waste samples (e.g., fruit peels, vegetable scraps, leaves, twigs)
- ☑ Soil
- ☑ Small gardening tools (shovels, gloves)
- ☑ Hand sanitizer

Lesson Duration:
1 HOUR

Steps to work through this lesson in real life

1. **Preparation:**

   ☐ **Gather all necessary materials**: picture book, compost bin or clear container, organic waste samples, soil, gardening tools and hand sanitizer.

   ☐ Set up the area where the lesson will take place, ensuring there is enough space for children to sit comfortably and participate in activities.

2. **Introduction (10 minutes)**

- ☐ **Welcome:** Gather children in a circle and introduce the topic of composting.

- ☐ **Discussion Starter:** Use questions to engage the children and get them thinking about waste and gardening.

- ☐ Ask questions like, "What do you think happens to apple cores or banana peels after we eat the fruit?" and "Have you ever helped in the garden at home?"

- ☐ **Story Time:** Read the book about composting to the children. This helps to visually introduce the concept in a simple and engaging way.

3. Explanation and Demonstration (15 minutes)

- ☐ **Explain composting in simple terms**: "Composting is turning leftover food and garden waste into rich soil that helps plants grow."

- ☐ **Show Samples**: Show different types of organic waste that can be composted, such as fruit peels, vegetable scraps, leaves, and twigs. Discuss what can and cannot be composted.

- ☐ **Mini-Compost Bin Demonstration**: Use a clear plastic container or small compost bin to demonstrate the steps of composting:

- ☐ **Layering**: Show how to create layers of green waste (e.g., fruit peels) and brown waste (e.g., leaves, twigs).

- ☐ **Adding Soil**: Add a layer of soil to help break down the waste faster.

4. Hands-On Activity (20 minutes)

Building a Mini-Compost Bin:

☐ **Step 1**: Let children take turns adding layers of green and brown waste to the bin.

☐ **Step 2**: Add soil to cover the waste.

☐ **Step 3**: Mix the layers gently with a small shovel or hands (wear gloves).

☐ **Mixing and Turning**: Show how to mix and turn the compost to help it decompose faster. Explain that this should be done every few days.

5. **Fun and Learning (10 minutes)**

☐ **Gardening Activity**: Let children plant seeds or small plants in the compost-enriched soil. Explain how compost helps plants grow strong and healthy.

6. **Wrap-Up and Review (5 minutes)**

☐ **Recap**: Review the key points: what composting is, what can be composted, and why it's important.

☐ **Q&A**: Allow children to ask questions about composting.

☐ **Take-Home Message**: Encourage children to share what they learned with their families and start composting at home if possible.

Activity Page

WHAT SCRAPS DO YOU SEE IN YOUR KITCHEN ON A DAILY BASIS? CAN YOU MAKE A LIST?

1. ____

2. ____

3. ____

4. ____

5. ____

6. ____

7. ____

8. ____

HOW CAN YOU HELP YOUR FAMILY AT HOME TO MAKE SURE THEY COMPOST?

DISCLAIMER:

This book is intended as a fun and educational
introduction to composting for children.
Please note that the author is not a professional composting
expert, and this book does not cover every aspect of the
composting process. While the information presented
is based on general principles, it is not exhaustive or a
substitute for professional advice. For detailed and specific
guidance on composting, please consult a knowledgeable
expert or trusted resources.

HAPPY COMPOSTING!